## DATE DUE

| | | | |
|---|---|---|---|
| AUG 17 '93 | MAR 07 '9 | FEB 08 '01 | |
| OCT 19 '93 | JUL 25 '96 | MAR 02 '01 | |
| OCT 25 '93 | OCT 18 '96 | DEC 12 '01 | |
| JAN 25 '94 | JAN 04 '97 | JAN 03 '02 | |
| FEB 26 '94 | JUL 11 '97 | MAR 01 '02 | |
| APR 12 '94 | JUL 24 | SEP 17 '02 | |
| JUN 16 '94 | MAY 14 '98 | OCT 24 '02 | |
| SEP 20 '94 | AUG 05 '99 | DEC 05 '02 | |
| NOV 19 '94 | OCT 21 | OCT 1 '03 | |
| DEC 13 '94 | FEB 23 '00 | NOV 19 '03 | |
| FEB 10 '95 | MAY 16 '00 | APR 06 | |
| APR 08 '95 | JUN 15 '00 | | |
| JUL 19 '95 | | | |
| GAYLORD | JUL 13 '00 | | PRINTED IN U.S.A. |

A Children's Book About

# COMPLAINING

Grolier Enterprises, Inc. offers a varied selection of children's
book racks and tote bags. For details on ordering, please write:
Grolier Enterprises Inc., Sherman Turnpike, Danbury, CT 06816
Attn: Premium Department

**Managing Editor: Ellen Klarberg**
**Copy Editor: Annette Gooch**
**Editorial Assistant: Lana Eberhard**
**Art Director: Jennifer Wiezel**
**Production Artist: Gail Miller**
**Illustration Designer: Bartholomew**
**Inking Artist: Linda Hanney**
**Coloring Artist: Linda Hanney**
**Lettering Artist: Linda Hanney**
**Typographer: Communication Graphics**

A Children's Book About

# COMPLAINING

## By Joy Berry

GROLIER ENTERPRISES CORP.

This book is about Amy and her friend Tami.

Reading about Amy and Tami can help you understand and deal with **complaining**.

You are complaining when you are not pleased with something and say so.

Complaining is saying that something is wrong. It is finding fault with something.

When you are with someone who keeps complaining:
- How do you feel?
- What do you think?
- What do you do?

When you are with someone who complains:

- You might feel unhappy and disappointed.
- You might think it is not fun to spend time with the person.
- You might decide you do not want to be around the person.

It is important to treat others the way you want to be treated.

If you do not want the people you are with to complain, you must not complain.

Too much complaining can make you feel bad.

It can cause you to think about the bad things around you instead of the good things.

Thinking about the bad things around you can put you in a bad mood.

When you are in a bad mood:
- You will probably have a bad day.
- You might say or do things that hurt you or the people and things around you.

Complaining can be harmful to you and others.

This does not mean you should keep quiet when something is really wrong. Sometimes you might need to complain.

Think before you complain. Complain only if it will help change something that needs to be changed.

Accept things as they are if they cannot be changed. Do not continue to complain.

When you need to complain:
- Do it in a nice way.
- Try not to shout.
- Try not to throw a tantrum.

When you must complain, try to suggest ways to solve the problem.

Once you are sure your complaint is understood, stop complaining.

Listen to what others have to say. If they suggest a good solution to the problem, follow it.

Remember to think about the good things around you. Talk about them.

Do not complain unless you need to.

It is important to treat people the way you want to be treated.

If you do not want others to complain around you, you must not complain around them.